UP DOWN
Early Concepts Skills

by Marilynn G. Barr

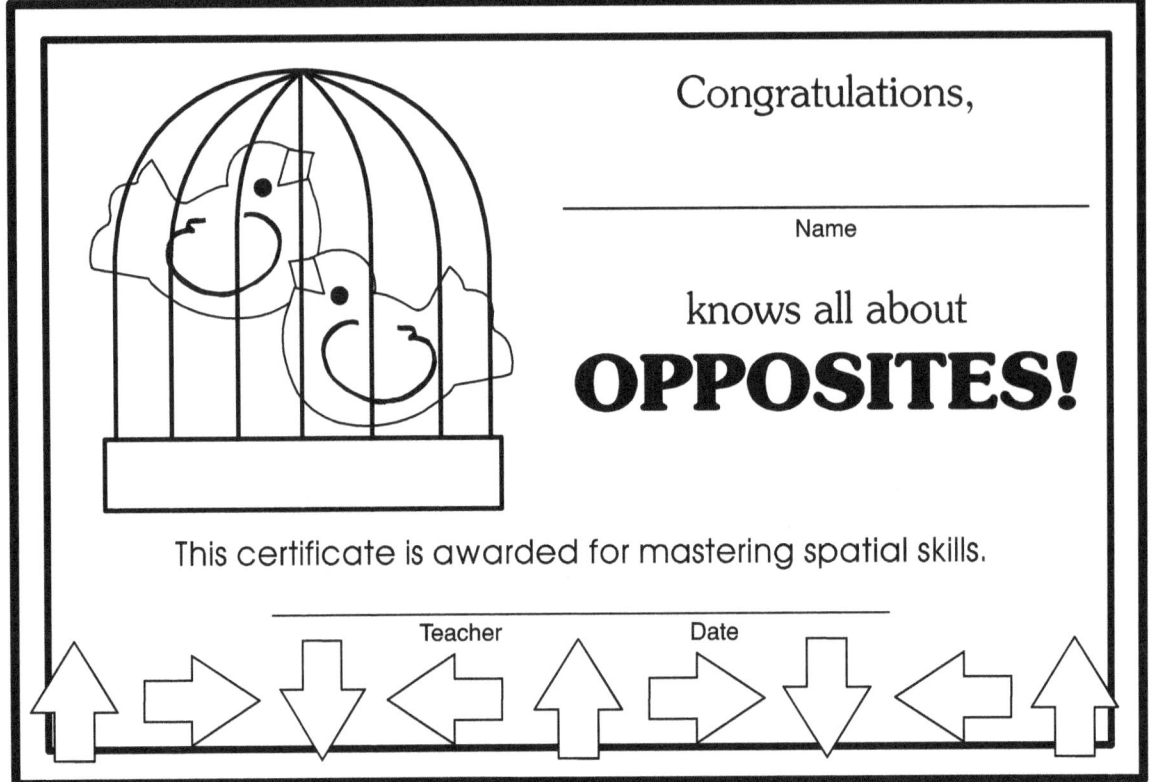

LAB20133
UP DOWN
by Marilynn G. Barr

Published by: Little Acorn Books™
Originally published by: Monday Morning Books, Inc.

Entire contents copyright © 2013 Little Acorn Books™

Little Acorn Books
PO Box 8787
Greensboro, NC 27419-0787

Promoting Early Skills for a Lifetime™

Little Acorn Books™
is an imprint of Little Acorn Associates, Inc.

http://www.littleacornbooks.com

Permission is hereby granted to reproduce student materials in this book for non-commercial individual or classroom use. *School-wide or system-wide use is expressly prohibited.

ISBN 978-1-937257-21-7

Printed in the United States of America

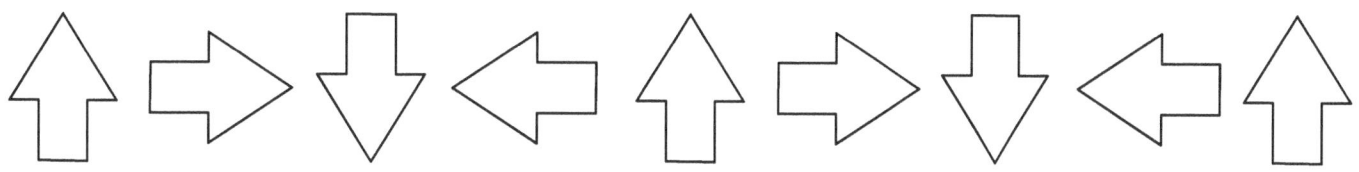

Up Down
Contents

Introduction..................................4
    Up Down Activities
    Up Down Hide and Seek
    Up Down Books
    Up Down Match Boards
    Up Down Displays
    Up Down Reviews
    Up Down Memory Card Game
    Up Down Puppets

Up Down Activities
    I Know Up and Down...................7
    I Know In and Out........................9
    I Know Inside and Outside..........11
    I Know Hot and Cold..................13
    I Know Wet and Dry...................14
    I Know Full and Empty................16
    I Know Open and Closed............18
    I Know Day and Night................20
    I Know Happy and Sad..............22
    I Know Front and Back..............23

I Know in Front and in Back..............25
I Know Small and Large....................26
I Know Under and Over....................28
I Know Old and New..........................29
I Know Hard and Soft........................31
I Know Left and Right........................32
I Know Same and Different..............34
Where Is the Cat?...............................36
Where Is the Mouse?........................38
Where Is the Dog?.............................40
Where Is the Frog?............................42
Where Is the Turtle?..........................44
Where Is the Chameleon?...............46
Where Is the Snowman?..................48

Hide and Seek
    House..50
    Tree..51
    Patterns.....................................52

Up Down Review................................55
Up Down Cards...................................61

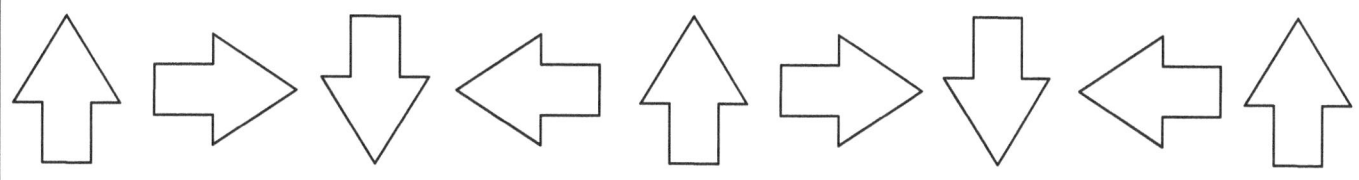

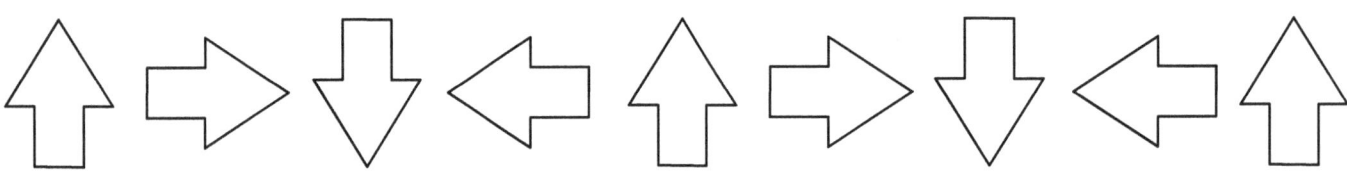

Up Down Introduction

Prepare children for a learning adventure with this collection of readiness skills activities. Up Down features skills practice for opposites and spatial concepts fun. Children color, cut out, and glue objects up and down, in and out, in front and in back, and more. Each activity is designed to help children develop fine motor skills through coloring, cutting, and pasting.

Assembly, materials, and alternate use options are listed at the bottom of activity pages. Children can glue on pom poms, sequins, beans, rice, cereal Os, and other decorations to add sparkle to their pictures.

Reinforce spatial concepts skills with Hide and Seek patterns. Children take turns arranging and guessing the spatial placement of objects and creatures. Encourage children to use spatial word clues and responses as they guess where objects or creatures are hidden. Hide and Seek patterns also offer early mapping skills practice. Children take turns mapping a scene as they follow oral spatial placement directions. Note: For young children, cut out the shapes and let the children glue them on the match board in the correct places.

Review pages and Up Down cards are also included.

Up Down Activities

Provide children with crayons, scissors, and glue to complete the activities. Two-page activities include patterns to cut out and glue on match boards. Children color, cut out, and glue patterns on the match boards. When children complete activities, invite each child to tell about his or her picture. Encourage children to use descriptive words. For example: The blue cat chased the gray mouse up on the roof.

The option at the bottom of an activity page suggests alternate materials and uses. Provide children with additional materials to create textured displays and more.

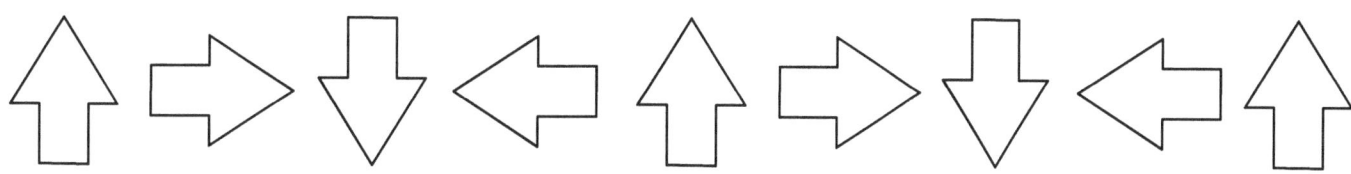

Up Down Hide and Seek

Reproduce the Hide and Seek patterns (pp. 50-54) for a spatial or mapping skills practice activity. Color, laminate, and cut out the patterns. Draw an outdoor scene on a sheet of poster board. Place the board on a table. To play Hide and Seek: Invite children, in turn, to arrange the patterns on the poster board, then identify and hide a specific object or creature somewhere in the scene. Have  the rest of the children take turns guessing where the creature or object is hidden. Encourage children to use spatial words when guessing "Is the dog under the bush?" For a mapping skills activity: Recite oral directions for children, in turn, to place patterns on the board. "Put the house in the center of the board." "Put the dog house on the left of the house."

Up Down Books

Provide children with construction paper, crayons, markers, scissors, and glue. Have children cut out and glue finished activities to sheets of construction paper to form book pages. Have children decorate construction paper covers for their books. Punch two holes along the left margin of each child's cover and book pages. Cut, lace, and tie a length of yarn or ribbon through the holes to form a book.

Up Down Match Boards

Enlarge, reproduce, color, and cut out each two-page activity. Example: I Know Up and Down (pp. 7-8). Tape or glue an envelope to the back of each match board for cutouts storage. Place the match boards in a center for individual or buddy skills practice.

Up Down Displays

Provide optional materials listed at the bottom of activity pages. Have children decorate, then cut out, and glue the pages on colored construction paper to make decorative displays. Punch two holes at the top of each picture. Cut, lace, and tie a length of yarn through the holes. Hang the displays in the classroom.

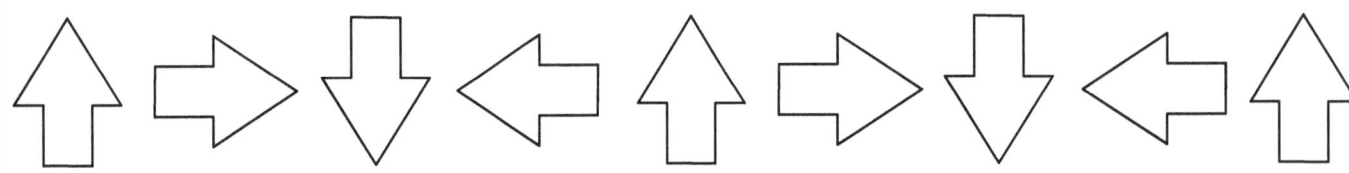

Up Down Reviews

Enlarge, reproduce, cut out, and glue each review page (pp. 55-60) to a sheet of construction paper. Laminate, then punch a hole in the top left corner. Lace and tie a length of yarn through the hole. Tie the loose end of the yarn around a wipe-off marker. Secure the yarn with tape. Children review what they have learned as they color or circle the pictures on each review sheet. Option: Instruct children to color or circle the pictures that are different or opposite from the first picture in each row.

Up Down Memory Card Game

Reproduce, color, laminate, and cut apart two sets of Up Down Cards (pp. 61-64). Store the cards in a decorated box or resealable storage bag. To play: One of two to four players shuffles, then places all the cards, face down, on a table. In turn, each child turns over two cards. If there is a match, the child takes the cards. If there is no match, the cards are turned face down and remain in the same locations. Play continues until all the cards are taken. Note: A match can be identical cards or opposite cards. Have children decide a match option before the game begins. For advanced skills practice, allow both match options during play.

Up Down Puppets

Reproduce the "I Know Front and Back" puppet patterns (pp. 23-24) for children to color and cut out. Help children tape the patterns together. Do not tape the bottom edge of patterns. Then glue or staple a large craft stick between the front and back patterns to form stick puppets.

I Know Up and Down

Color one cat orange, one cat blue, and one cat red.
Color one mouse pink, one mouse brown, and one mouse gray.
Cut out the cats and the mice.

Option: Reproduce the cats and mice on colored construction paper or transfer to felt, cloth scraps, or gift wrap.

I Know Up and Down

Glue the blue cat and the gray mouse up on the roof.
Glue the orange cat and the red cat down on the ground.
Glue the pink mouse and the brown mouse down on the ground.
Color the rest of the picture.

Option: Glue orange yarn scraps on the cat outlines. Glue brown and white pom poms on the mice outlines. Then draw features on the cats and the mice.

I Know In and Out

Color one bird orange.
Color one bird purple.
Color one bird green.
Cut out the birds.

Option: Glue craft feathers on each bird.

I Know In and Out

Glue one bird in the cage.
Glue one bird out on the table.
Glue the flying bird out of the cage.
Color the rest of the picture.

Option: Trace, cut out, and glue felt birds on the picture.

I Know Inside and Outside

Color one dog and one cat purple.
Color one dog and one cat orange.
Cut out the cats and dogs.

Option: Color and cut out the cats and dogs. Glue or tape a craft stick to the back of each cutout to form a stick puppet.

I Know Inside and Outside

Glue a dog inside each dog house.
Glue a cat outside each dog house.
Color the picture.

Option: Cut out and glue pictures of dogs and cats from magazines.

I Know Hot and Cold

Look at the picture.
Color the cold objects blue.
Color the hot objects red.
Color the rest of the picture.

Option: Color, cut out, and glue this page to the front of a construction paper booklet. Cut pictures of hot and cold objects from magazines. Glue the pictures in the booklet.

I Know Wet and Dry

Color the raindrops blue.
Color the dolls.
Cut out the dolls.

Option: Paint watercolor raindrops on the picture.

I Know Wet and Dry

Look at the picture.
Glue the wet doll in the rain.
Glue the dry doll under the umbrella.
Color the picture.

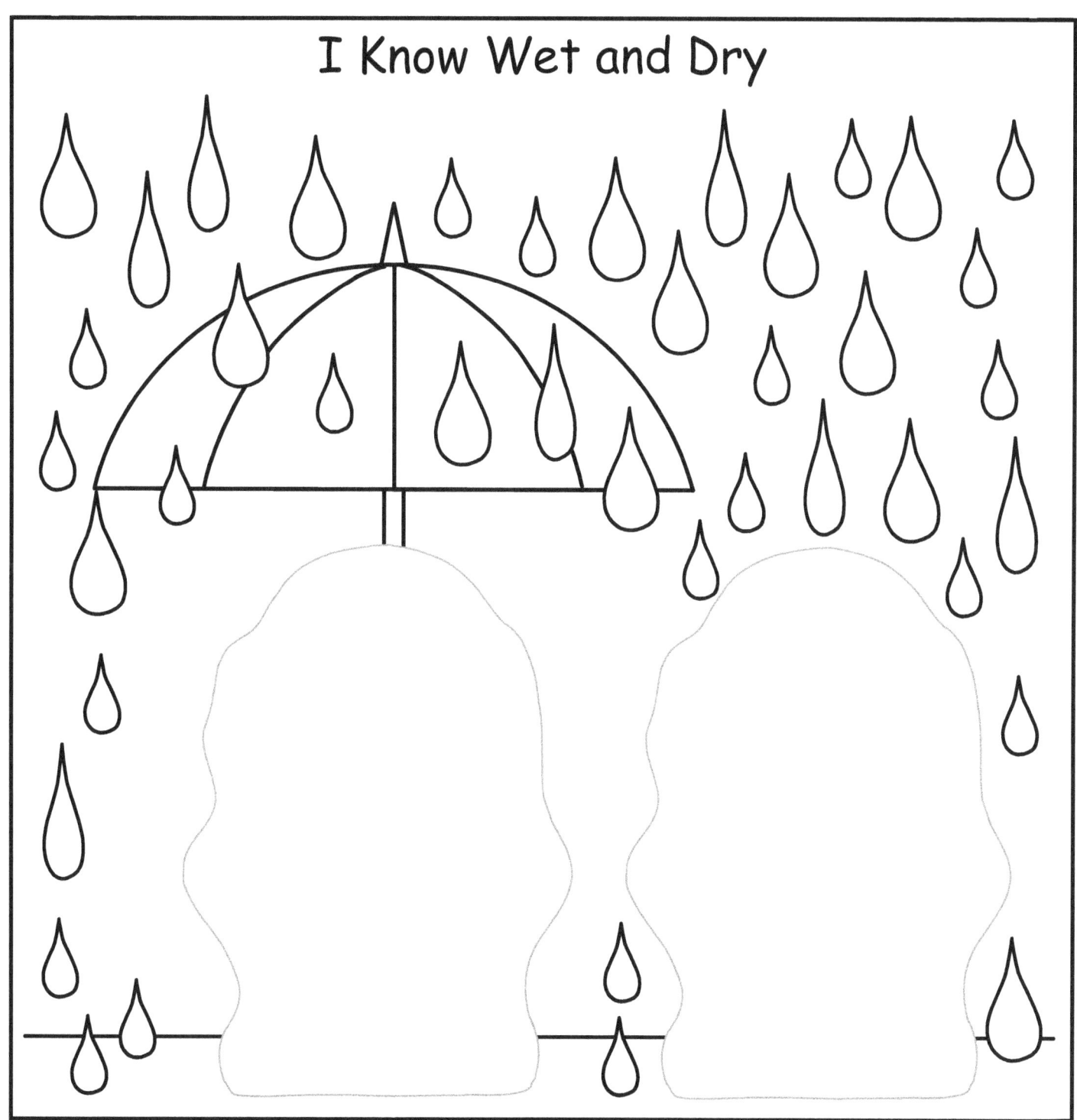

Option: Color the raindrops with glitter pens.

I Know Full and Empty

Look at the jars.
Are the jars full or empty?
Draw jelly beans in three jars.
How many jars are now full? How many jars are now empty?

Option: Glue on small pom poms, beads, and buttons to fill up the jars.

I Know Full and Empty

Look at the picture.
Color the empty containers green.
Color the full containers orange.

Option: Glue cereal Os, beans, and beads on the empty containers.

I Know Open and Closed

Look at the buildings.
Color the open doors yellow.
Color the closed doors orange.
Color the rest of the picture.

Option: Paint on glue, then sprinkle sand on the walls.

I Know Open and Closed

Look at the objects on each shelf.
Color the open objects green.
Color the closed objects blue.

I Know Day and Night

Look at the picture.
Color the cat in the day picture yellow.
Color the cat in the night picture brown.
Color the rest of the picture

Option: Measure, cut, and glue fabric curtains on the sides of each window.

I Know Day and Night

Look at the pictures.
Draw a moon in the night pictures.
Draw a sun in the day pictures.
Color the pictures.

Option: Glue a yellow pom pom sun on the day pictures. Glue a cotton ball moon on the night pictures.

I Know Happy and Sad

Look at the clowns.
Color the sad clowns blue.
Color the happy clowns orange.
Color the rest of the clowns.

Option: Glue a small pom pom at the top of each clown's hat.

I Know Front and Back

Color the puppet patterns.
Cut out the puppet patterns.
Glue a craft stick between the cutouts.

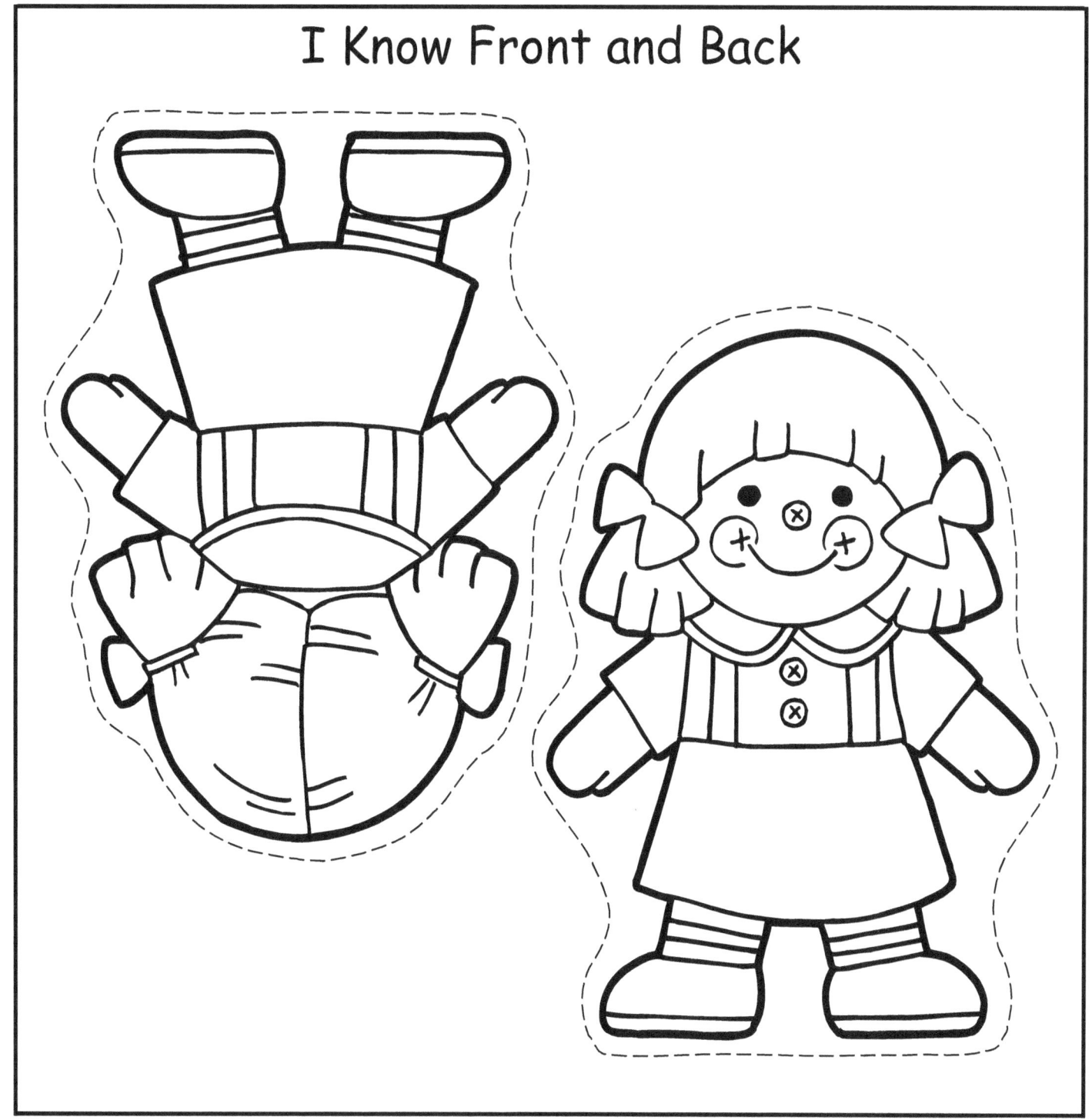

Option: Glue puppet cutouts on each side of a small paper bag to form hand puppets.

I Know Front and Back

Color the puppet patterns.
Cut out the puppet patterns.
Glue a craft stick between the cutouts.

Option: Glue buttons and yarn hair on the puppet.

I Know in Front and in Back

Look at the pictures.
Color the mice in front pink.
Color the mice in back gray.
Color the cheese yellow. Color the butterflies blue.

Option: Glue yellow glitter on the cheese.

I Know Small and Large

Look at the creatures in the picture.
Color the small creatures green.
Color the large creatures blue.
Cut out the creatures .

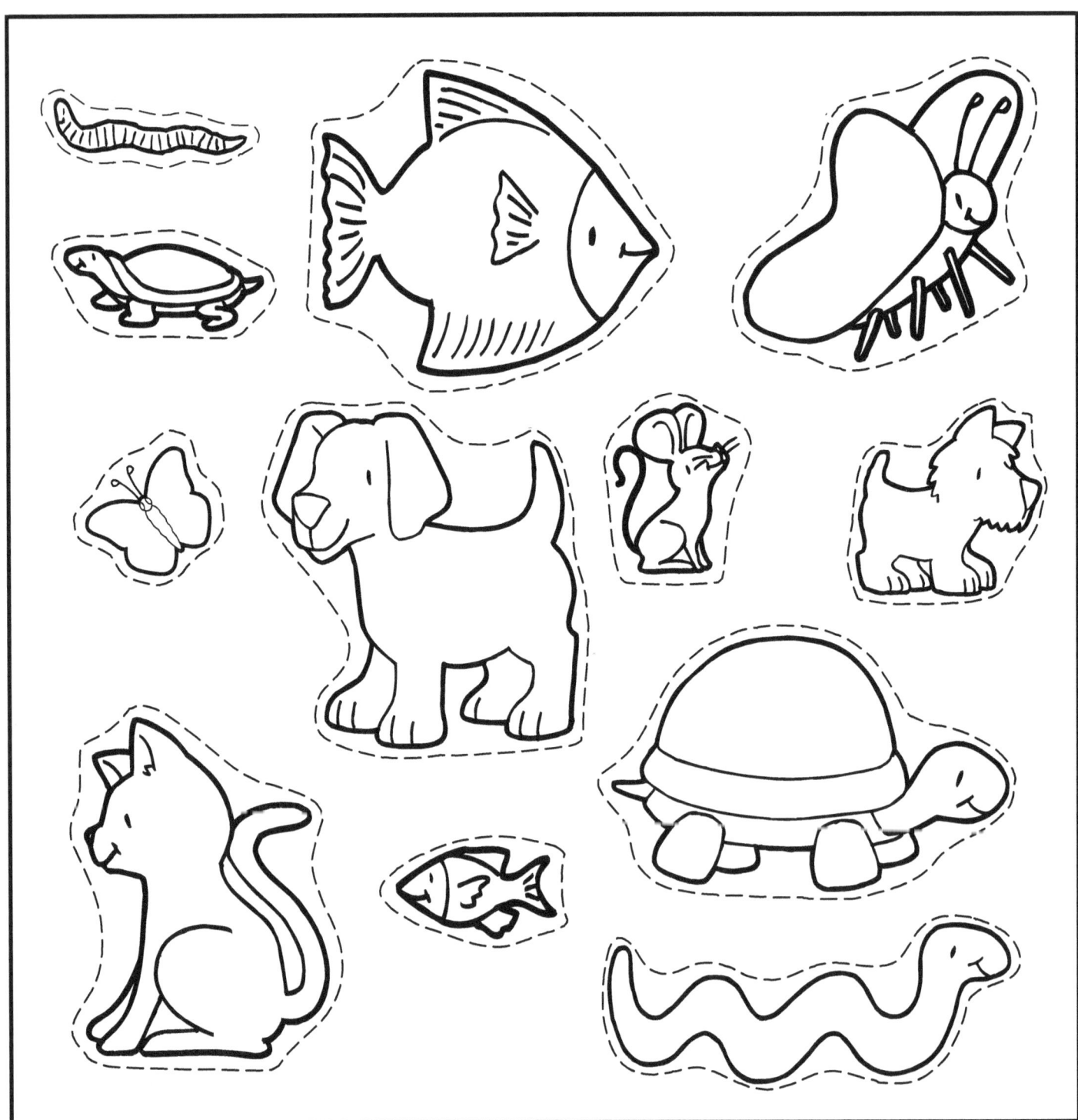

Option: Color, cut out, and glue the patterns on a sheet of construction paper. Glue on buttons, craft tissue scraps, and cereal Os to create a collage.

I Know Small and Large

Glue the small animals at the top of the box.
Glue the large animals in the bottom of the box.

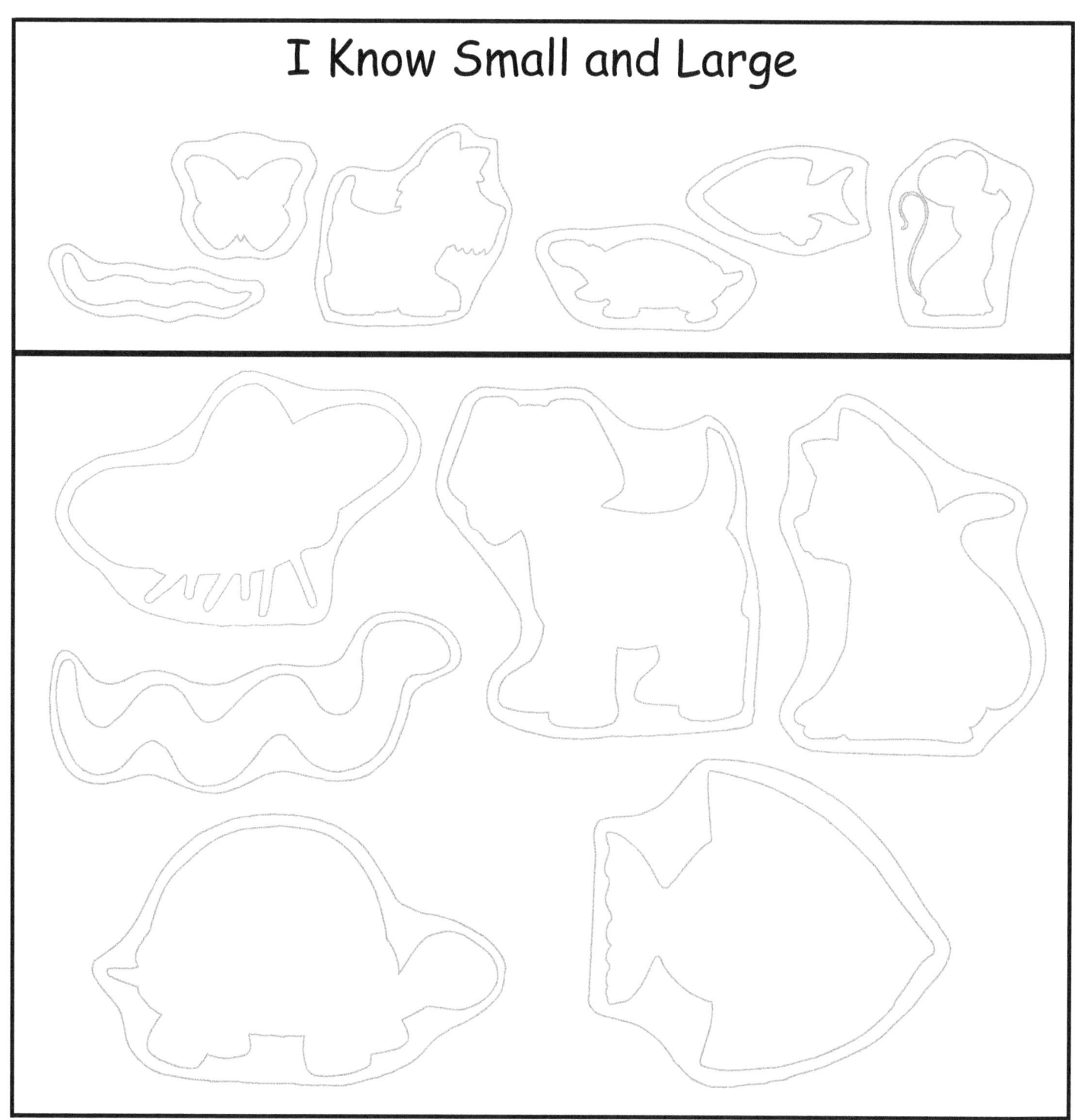

Option: Use the patterns to create a pet store picture.

I Know Under and Over

Look at the pictures.
Color the bees flying over the beehives yellow.
Color the bees flying under the beehives orange.
Color the beehives brown.

Option: Glue cereal Os on the beehives.

I Know Old and New

Color the old hats purple.
Color the new hats red.
Cut out the hats.

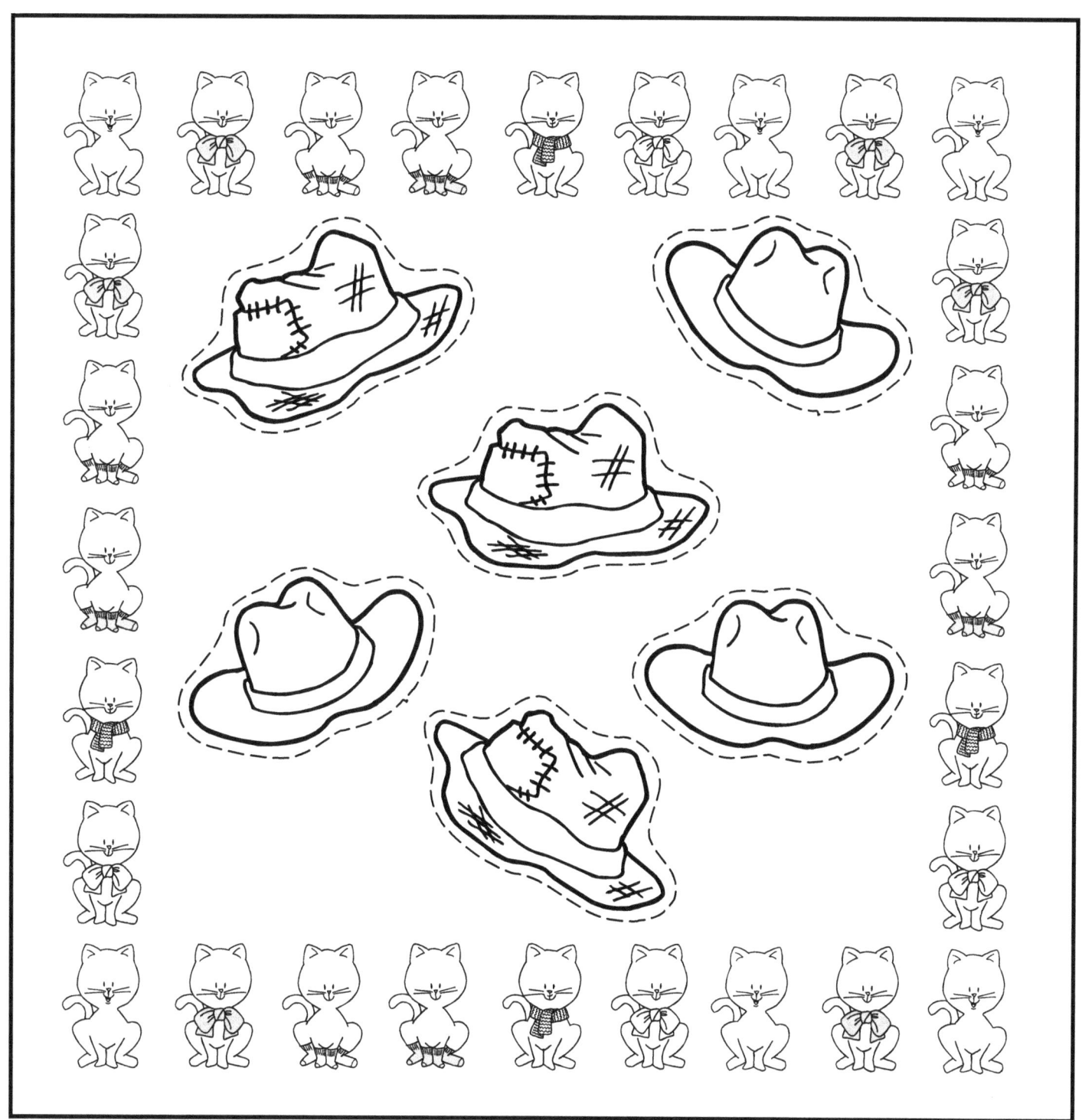

Option: Draw six funny creatures on a sheet of construction paper. Color, cut out, and glue a hat on each creature.

I Know Old and New

Glue an old hat on each cat wearing socks.
Glue a new hat on each cat wearing a bow.
Are all of the cats wearing hats?
Color the picture.

Option: Use glitter sticks to draw old and new hats on the cats.

I Know Hard and Soft

Color the soft objects pink.
Color the hard objects brown.
Color the rest of the objects blue.

Option: Use a crayon to draw a circle around each soft object.

I Know Left and Right

Color the beach ball red and the baseball blue.
Color the top orange.
Color the yo-yo purple.
Cut out the patterns.

Option: Draw a toy box on a sheet of construction paper. Color, cut out, and glue the toys in the toy box.

I Know Left and Right

Glue the beach ball on the right side of the cat.
Glue the baseball on the left side of the cat.
Glue the yo-yo in the left pocket.
Glue the top in the right pocket.

Option: Cut out and glue pictures of objects from magazines on each outline.

I Know Same and Different

Look at the cakes in each row.
Color the cakes that are the same pink.
Color the cakes that are different blue.

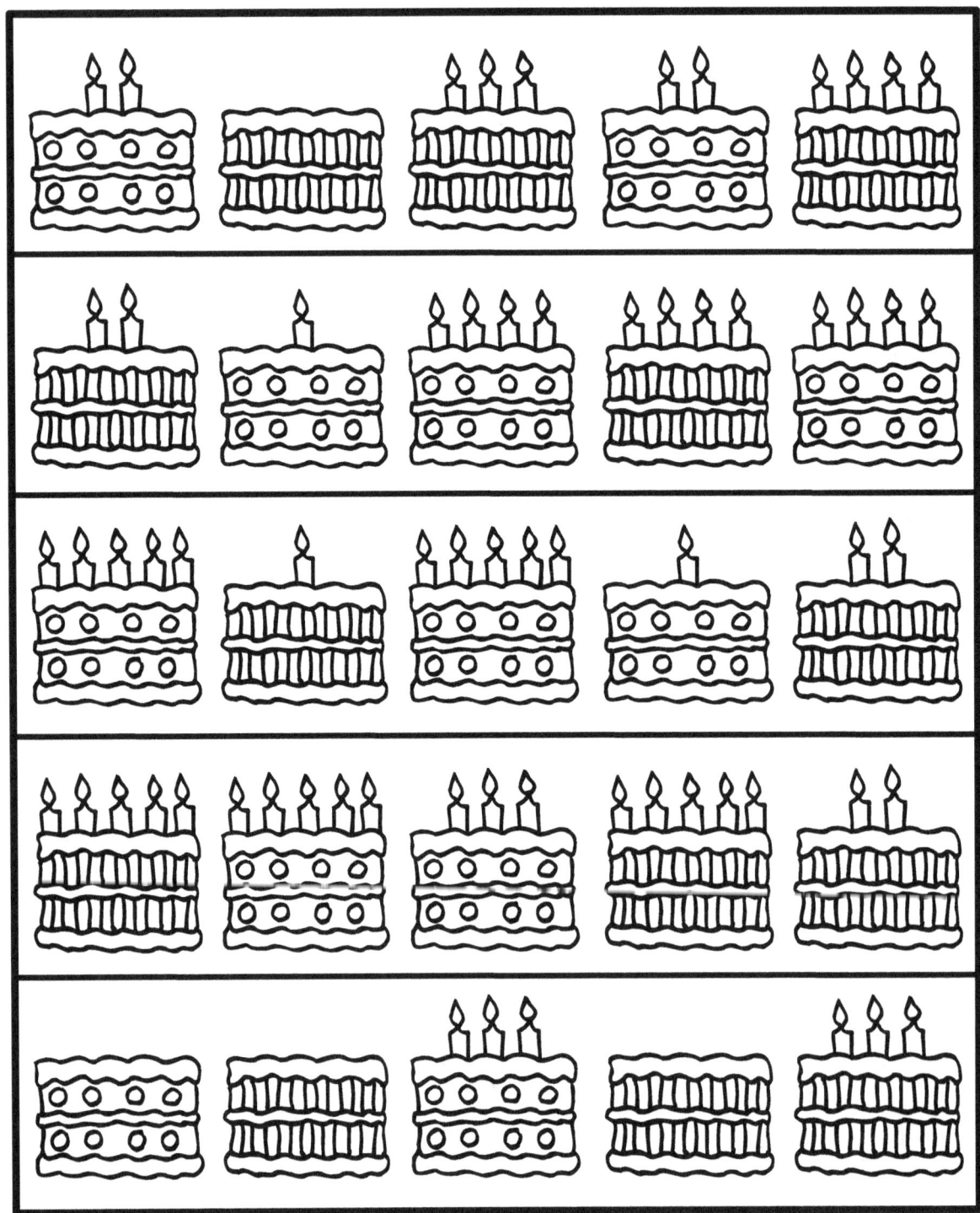

Option: Cut apart each row of cakes to use as bookmarks.

I Know Same and Different

Look at the cats in each row.
Color the cat that is different orange.
Color the cats that are the same purple.

Option: Color, cut out, and punch a hole in each cat. Measure, cut, lace, and tie a necklace-length of yarn though the hole in each cat to form a necklace.

Where Is the Cat?

Color the patterns.
Cut out the patterns along the dotted lines.

Option: Glue green pom poms on the turtle. Glue orange pom poms on the pumpkin. Glue yellow pom poms on the cat. Trace, cut out, and glue a gift wrap shade on the lamp.

Where Is the Cat?

Look at the outlines.
Glue the matching shape pattern on each outline.
Color the picture.

Where is the cat?

Option: Glue cotton balls on the clouds in the sky.

Where Is the Mouse?

Color the patterns.
Cut out the patterns along the dotted lines.

Option: Color, cut out, and glue the patterns on a sheet of construction paper. Write a story about the mouse, the turtle, and the cat along the bottom.

Where Is the Mouse?

Look at the outlines.
Glue the matching shape pattern on each outline.
Color the picture.

Where is the mouse?

Option: Paint on glue, then sprinkle the window panes with glitter.

Where Is the Dog?

Color the patterns.
Cut out the patterns along the dotted lines.

Option: Color, cut out, and staple or glue a craft stick to the back of each pattern to form stick puppets and props.

Where Is the Dog?

Look at the outlines.
Glue the matching shape pattern on each outline.
Color the picture.

Where is the dog?

Option: Cut out and glue a picture of an object from a magazine or an old greeting card on each outline.

Where Is the Frog?

Color the patterns.
Cut out the patterns along the dotted lines.

Option: Color, cut out, and glue the frog and yarn ball on a sheet of construction paper. Write a story about the frog and the yarn ball.

Where Is the Frog?

Look at the outlines.
Glue the matching shape pattern on each outline.
Color the picture.

Where is the frog?

Option: Draw a plant in the basket.

Where Is the Turtle?

Color the patterns.
Cut out the patterns along the dotted lines.

Option: Measure, cut, and assemble an oak tag headband. Color, cut out, and glue the patterns around the headband.

Where Is the Turtle?

Look at the outlines.
Glue the matching shape pattern on each outline.
Color the picture.

Where is the turtle?

Option: Draw the sun up in the sky.

Where Is the Chameleon?

Color the patterns.
Cut out the patterns along the dotted lines.

Option: Color, cut out, and glue a craft stick to the back of each pattern.

Where Is the Chameleon?

Look at the outlines.
Glue the matching shape pattern on each outline.
Color the picture.

Where is the chameleon?

Option: Cut out and glue a picture of an object from a magazine or an old greeting card on each outline.

Where Is the Snowman?

Color the patterns.
Cut out the patterns along the dotted lines.

Option: Color, cut out, and glue a craft stick to the back of each pattern.

Where Is the Snowman?

Look at the shape outlines.
Glue the matching shape patterns on the outlines.
Color the rest of the picture.

Option: Use silver glitter glue to make the snowman sparkle.

Hide and Seek House

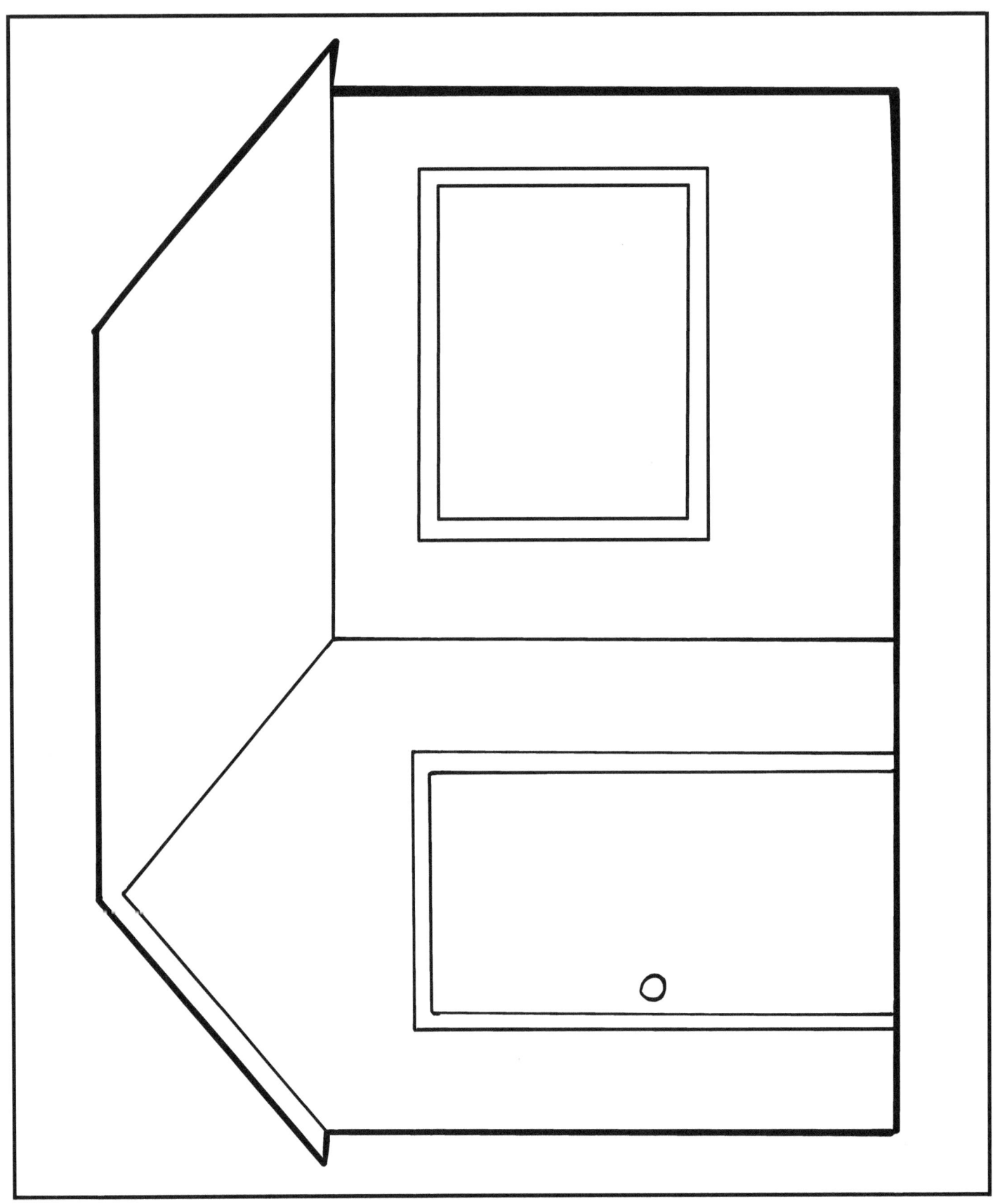

Option: Decorate the house with gift wrap, tissue paper, or construction paper.

Hide and Seek Tree

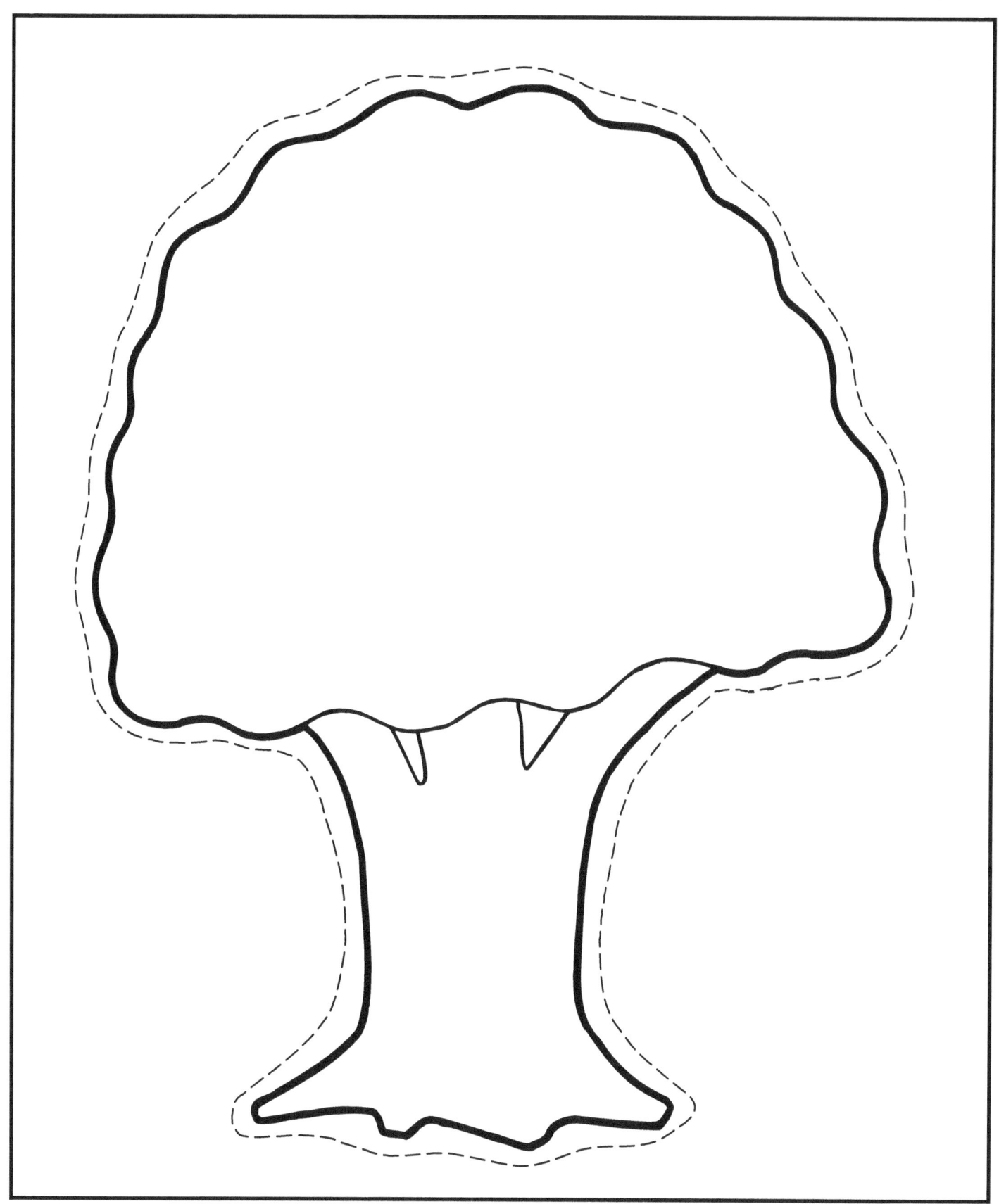

Option: Tear and glue green tissue paper leaves on the tree.

Hide and Seek Patterns

Option: Cut and glue or tape blue cellophane to the pond. Glue a pom pom in the center of each flower.

Hide and Seek Patterns

Swing

Option: Trace, color, and cut out a brown grocery bag dog house. Glue buttons, beans, or pom poms in the box.

Hide and Seek Patterns

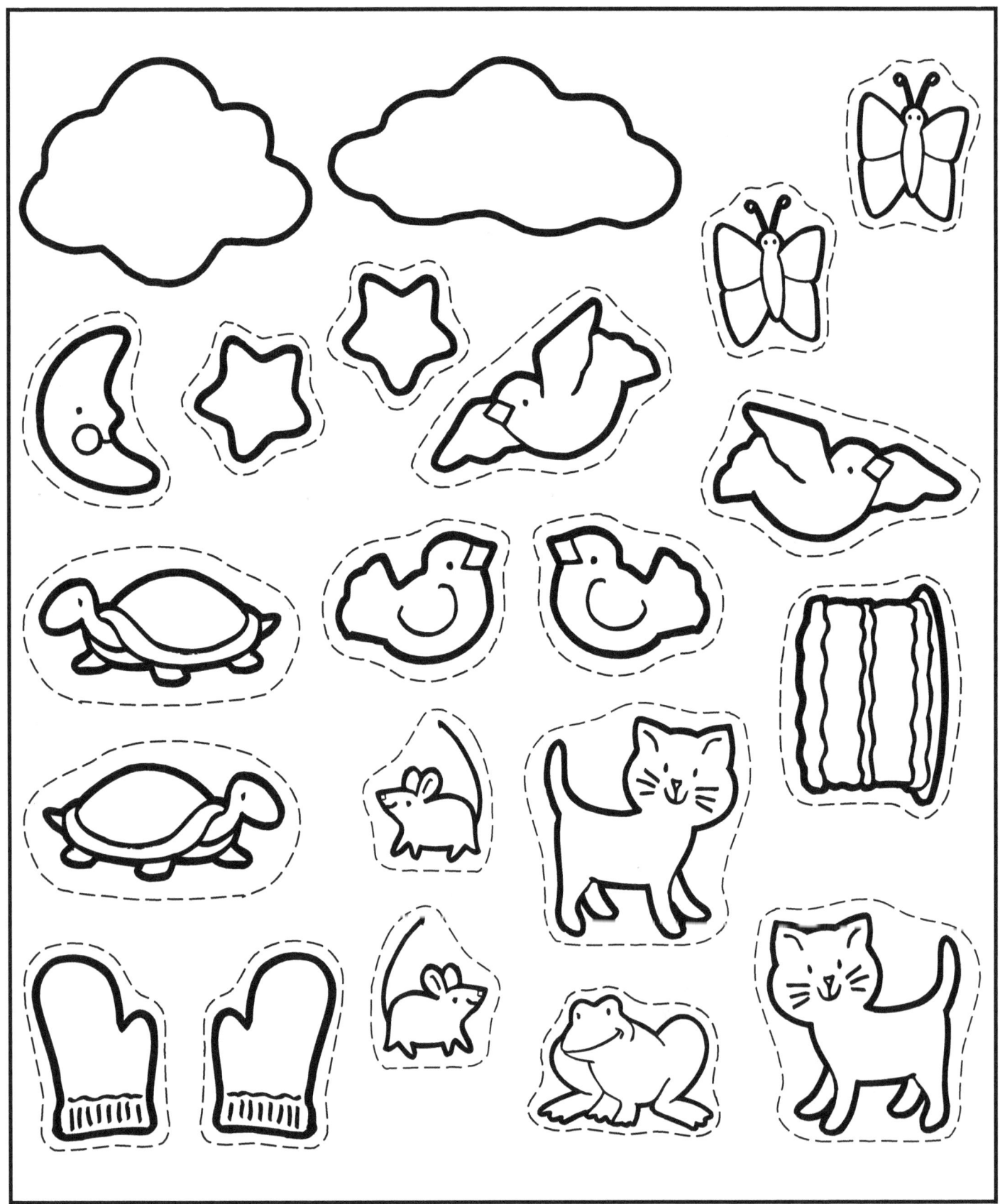

Option: Reproduce these patterns from colored construction paper or craft foam.

Up Down Review

Look at the pictures.
Color the pictures that match the first picture in each row red.

Up Down Review

Look at the pictures.
Color the pictures that match the first picture in each row blue.

big	
little	
full	
empty	
hot	
cold	

Up Down Review

Look at the pictures.
Color the pictures that match the first picture in each row purple.

Up Down Review

Look at the pictures.
Color the pictures that match the first picture in each row green.

Up Down Review

Look at the pictures.
Color the pictures that match the first picture in each row orange.

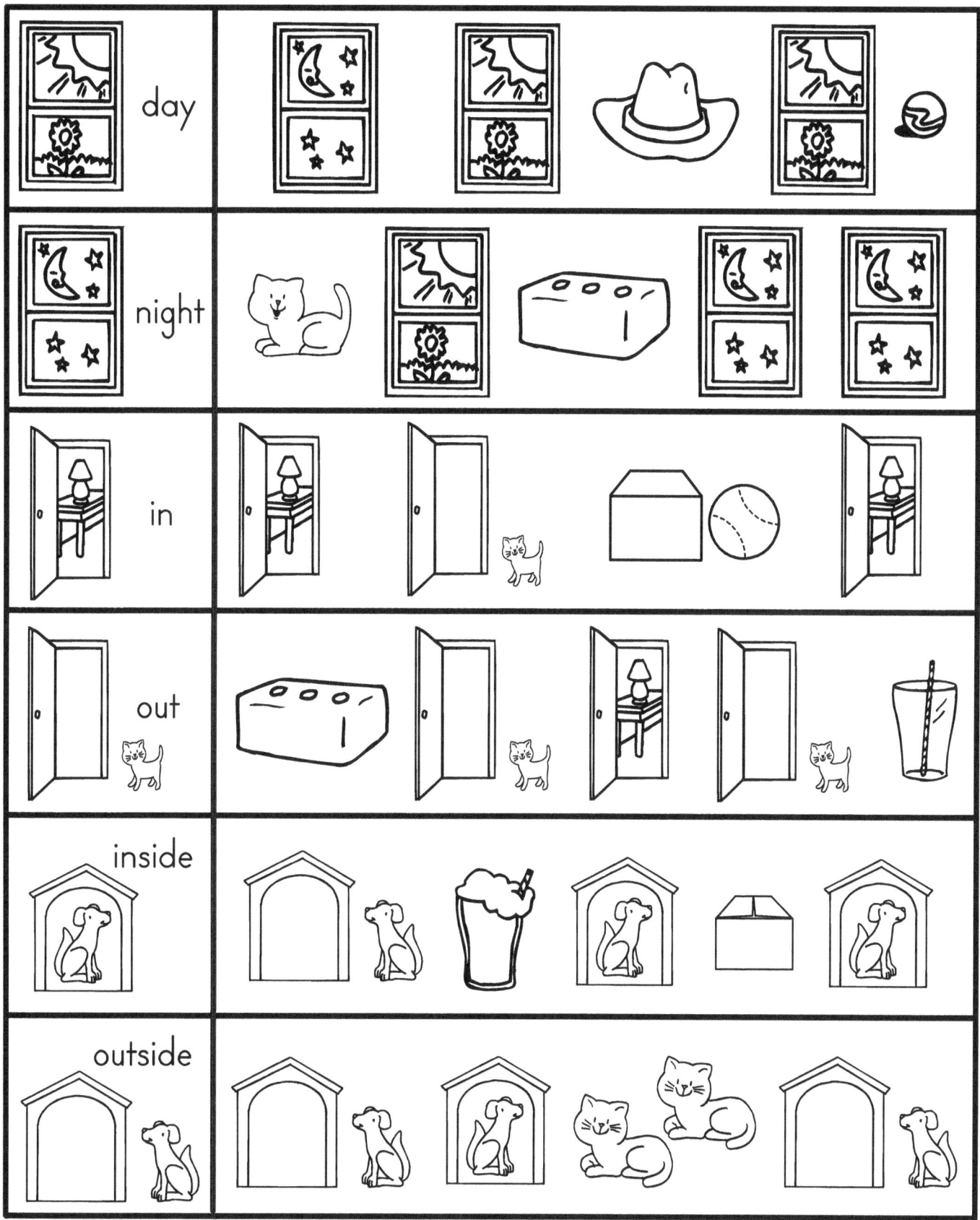

Up Down Review

Look at the pictures.
Color the pictures that match the first picture in each row yellow.

front						
back						
same						
different						
open						
closed						

Up Down Cards

front 	back 	hard 
soft 	wet 	dry 
same 	different 	open 

Up Down Cards

closed	left	right
up	down	big
little	in front	in back

LAB20133 • UP DOWN • 972-1-937257-21-7 ©2013 Little Acorn Books™

Up Down Cards

full	empty	old
new	happy	sad
under	over	hot

Up Down Cards

cold	in	out
inside	**outside**	**day**
night	**on**	**next to**

www.ingramcontent.com/pod-product-compliance
Lightning Source LLC
Chambersburg PA
CBHW081021040426
42444CB00014B/3304